Frédéric Delalot

2044
washingtonias and zoetropes 21

KDP Editions

Under the blue lights...

Centuries had passed...

Stories became other stories

A very long time ago

White plaster paths

Between the trees...

Tall grass...

Imagining a world...

Watching for the arrival of beings.

There were afternoons...

Improbably quiet

Multitude of music...

Then other gardens...

After the austere conflict...

New souls were coming...

Endlessly...

And the city, in the distance, was waiting for us

That was the preamble...

Blades...

Where the certainties basked

Hypersport...

Undulations in the night

Every creature...

We could see their story...

And their rebirth...

Billions of things

At the heart of the world...

The moment...

The new days...

In the past, I was passing by

And I imagined the sequel...

Perfect happiness...

Achievements...

History of emotions...

And frolic...

By innocuous touches...

And I fit into those possibilities.

Grain of ecstasy...

Millennium door

On the heights

The wheel...

Wealth...

It's that I probably had the taste

From the fertile night

Next to a text...

Representation...

Where the assumptions were going?

Acquiescences...

In the decor...

Formidable...

To smile at the romantic image

Cosmopolitan...

Like this...

As an ambition...

Forests, high mountains...

The world on the way...

A story was invented...

Coming and going of enjoyment.

She kept boots

Attractive...

Shared her desires...

Euphoric sensations...

I was relaxing in the booth

Between the fabrics...

Under the stars...

In the world...

Through the ages...

In the present...

Ally of time...

Magic of power

Choosing existences...

There were swings

Bright...

That we heard...

3

In a hurry

Ideas

Elsewhere...

The city watered us

Dancing...

Caverns of screens...

I saw races

From that time...

With the landscapes...

These eras slumbered

For a second...

Becoming perspectives...

Looks...

Hopes...

In the spheres

Blue...

Continent...

Invisible until then...

Awakened by the rounds...

Meditative...

Through the snowy streets.

I was crossing the park...

Empty pools...

Illuminated by a halo

Thousands of worlds...

Cities...

Memories

Dried leaves

Kingdoms...

Accustomed to the polar skies

Noctilucent clouds...

In the mesosphere...

Illuminated the city...

Summer...

Methane emissions...

High atmosphere...

Sparkling blue glows.

Eroticism on hold

Fantasized...

To the city center...

I watched her dance

Haphazardly...

Fluid caresses...

Sometimes...

Interfering...

A detachment.

Random color...

Snippets of conversations...

Screens, back and forth

Harmless views...

The cars were firing...

Sadness and joy...

Years passed...

She had only a simple adornment

At leisure...

All night...

We were trained...

By the unreal images.

From a view...

Esplanade...

Like horses

In some street...

Still elsewhere...

To continue...

It was late to fall asleep...

As in the time of travel

Halo of buildings...

Aerial train...

By erasing stations

At high speed...

Accords of illusions

Kilometers...

And the passages...

Lyrical...

I loved tomorrow

New Year's Eve...

Orange, Hispanic...

Total freedom

Out of the way, drifts...

Long walks...

The city of simple joys

And at the feast of thoughts...

Distant landscapes...

Soothing wills...

The sap of ancient times

Again and again...

Remains of the nights...

White...

Hugs...

We carried the gold, our evenings...

The steps put the weeks to sleep

Mists...

Wrapped in stories...

And days and days

Nights and nights...

I was listening

The tirades

And the open sea...

Improvised

Feathers...

Sailor's sweaters

Matches...

From New York...

We had known each other

In Paris...

At the beginning of summer...

The brilliance of silences...

Moments of indifference

Gypsies...

Her breasts...

In the corners...

Chance of heights

From the microcosm...

Attractive...

As long as our bodies were getting drunk

Mind-blowing ships...

Between the tones of the trees...

Free conviction...

These nuances...

Things were on their own.

We stuck to the source

From our thoughts...

Off the merry-go-round...

Wild liqueur of the flowerbeds...

Such slow limits

The unfinished target...

Vegetable...

And the horizons...

In space-time...

Happiness of a few hours...

We loved each other...

With nothing but our impulses.

Galaxies were moving away

Strings of movement...

At the limits...

Erotic reality...

Other Bohemian outfits

Transparent...

Paces...

Flights of flight...

I wish the pleasure was eternal

That it was like beauty...

Landscapes...

We didn't want to stop shooting...

Excitations...

From the present moment...

In the strangeness of time

Story One...

The years had gone by...

As we abused these fields

Unreal...

Hypothetical worlds

Far away bottles...

Of an expanse ...

Of a perfect rhythm...

Where the atmosphere was pure

And quiet principles.

The track opened onto seas...

Idle...

Ageless...

Raw material of the full sequences

Slow mirages...

From a rhythm...

Years passed

Over there...

Republic

Royalty...

Treasure...

Priceless.

Everything had seemed far away

Like this...

Invincible seasons...

Hot...

We were always different

Of ourselves...

In the vast space...

Things went on...

Return of a principle

First...

Huge sails...

Magnetic paths

Which we managed to see

The contours...

And we were together...

Apart...

Along the ancient beaches

At dawn...

Lifting the sand...

Gold of the naves

Glorious

Elixirs...

Adventures...

Lyrical color

Arts...

Luminous ride

At night...

Sensual lips...

Firs...

Towers would be erected

New thoughts...

From ancient times...

Manufacturing...

She looked like one of those actresses.

Films by Roy Stuart...

Instinctive singing...

Special atmosphere...

Fleeting moment...

Caresses dominated the starts...

Gave the breaks the look of a party

Freedom game...

Agile speed...

Her fragrance left...

The memory of a gesture

For a few hours...

I was back on the road

The course of things...

Translucent...

Cosmic corridor...

Multicolored

Screen...

Games...

In the evening...

Library

From this island...

From the universe...

Tours...

In the evening...

Some atmosphere

From the time...

Exciting mystery...

Back to attractions.

Perhaps other desires were getting drunk

We played our roles instinctively...

Boudoir orgasms...

Where the magical force lasted...

Sketching other dreams...

Beyond metamorphosis

Loves, stories...

We sometimes noticed...

Attachments...

We had shared the essentials...

Naked, against each other...

In the perfect harmony of impulses.

Carried away by our desires

Pleasant drifts...

Through the hours...

And through the ages...

Old pontoons...

Of a strange love...

Worlds, then...

Created parentheses

In the unusual darkness...

The story had to be fluid

Between us...

The energy was traveling...

Facets of a desire...

Which confessed only at times...

Chapters already written, no doubt...

Closer to reality every time.

The color...

Of the moment

Tonnaged...

Counters...

And marquees...

Tall sparkling fir trees

Soundtrack...

Hypnotic...

Geometric elements.

The towers of the city center stood out

In the evening of possibilities...

Brown fir branches...

Bright...

Passages and expectations...

Speed of hours...

Walking up and down the street

Emotion...

How hastened I was...

In a half-sleep

Jacket...

Scarf...

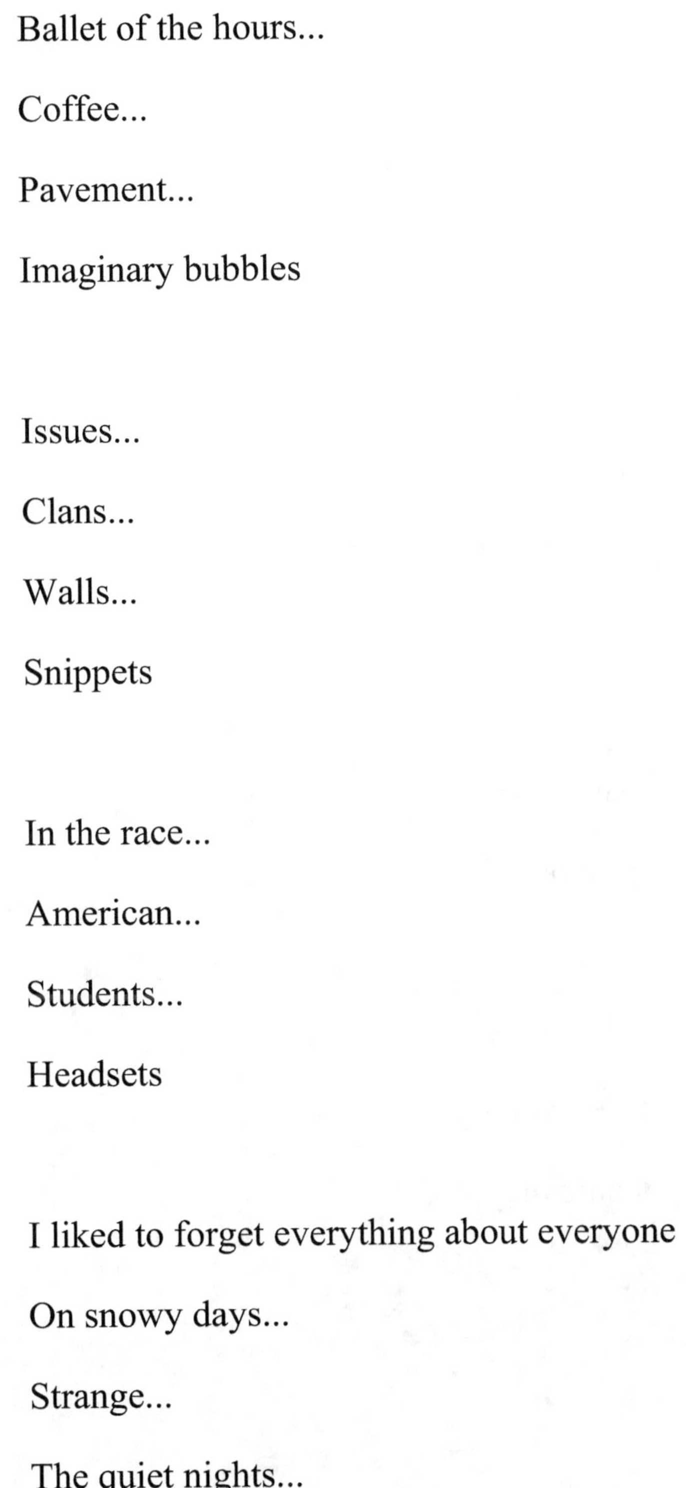

Ballet of the hours...

Coffee...

Pavement...

Imaginary bubbles

Issues...

Clans...

Walls...

Snippets

In the race...

American...

Students...

Headsets

I liked to forget everything about everyone

On snowy days...
Strange...
The quiet nights...

Long sequence

On the paths...

Waiting evenings

Eyes met

Dance theatre...

Potions...

Moments...

Of a mystery

Confusing...

When the Work had begun

All resources...

Available...

Then the sources themselves

They were already considering the project

Global...

The plot...

Earth's atmosphere...

Exploration...

From canyons...

Average depth

To the west and east...

In the quadrangles...

First of all programs

Training...

On the two moons...

Surface of the planet...

Robots would charge

To draw resources...

To create...

Off-center base...

With others...

High-altitude platform

Advanced beings...

They had often come...

Communicated telepathically

Kind of friendship...

Mutual understanding...

Tiny headphones...

Translucent...

Ancient Land Classics

All the leaves are brown

And the sky is grey...

I've been for a walk...

Supreme links...

Havens...

Our caresses, trophies.

Creative hobby...

Fantasies...

And meaning...

Constantly rejuvenated appearance

They were passing through misty parks

Intoxicating alleys of purple trees...

The intoxication of departures...

Sheets of spheres, spinning...

Flight hours...

Astronauts...

Asteroid near the Moon...

Before the Martian expedition.

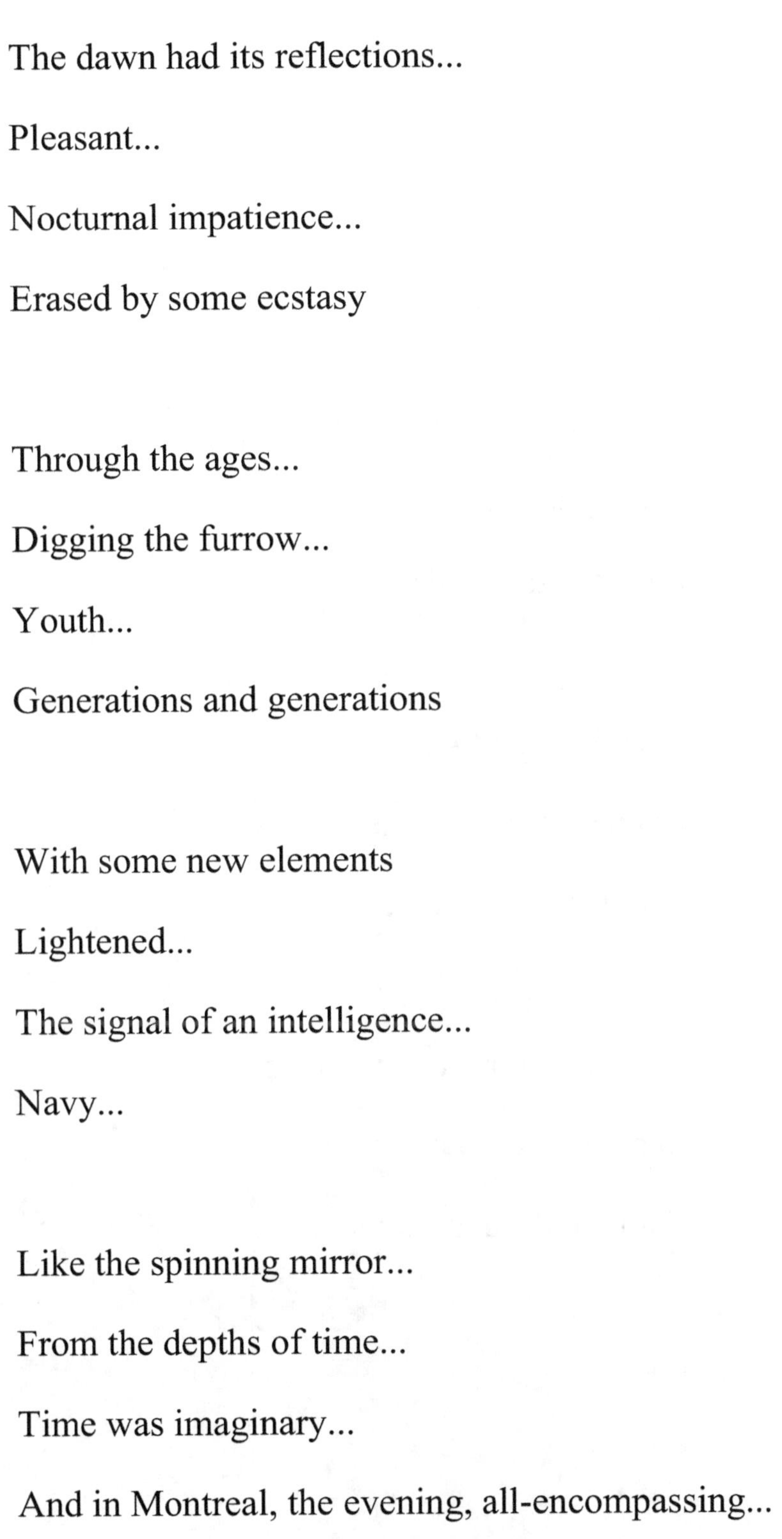

The dawn had its reflections...

Pleasant...

Nocturnal impatience...

Erased by some ecstasy

Through the ages...

Digging the furrow...

Youth...

Generations and generations

With some new elements

Lightened...

The signal of an intelligence...

Navy...

Like the spinning mirror...

From the depths of time...

Time was imaginary...

And in Montreal, the evening, all-encompassing...

Deep down, she loved dates.

Other years...

Between the reeds...

Then in the city...

From another continent

For other holidays...

Get drunk for a few minutes

Deciding not to be naked...

Game of desires shown...

And she would like to play

Nonchalance...

Choosing the rhythm...

Attractions...

Youth interfering

In desire...

Endless excitement

Nights across the massif

Starry sky of nights...

Repetitive...

Era, see parties

At the other windows...

Seeing paintings...

Sculptures of the apartments

Virgos...

A kingdom...

The air of the years...

Rates...

Strange alchemy...

We spoke in their ears

Movement strings

At the limits...

Edge of the moons...

External...

Dawn...

Statues...

From the moon...

Of creation.

Eccentric position...

The sea, back-to-school, distance

Discreet illusions...

Nights were passing...

A tower on the horizon

One summer...

In the aftermath...

From an evening...

We wanted to trace.

Quick patterns...

From place to place...

Frescoes of a summer...

Reach the beaches

Night...

Unknowns...

By the way, Hindu tunes

Night of spaces...

Postures...

Adorning the dawns...

We had a drink...

Another night or maybe the same night.

Young...

In another era...

I had lived for some time in accelerated

Thoroughly in Ford...

We went out a lot...

We slept little...

Desires in the moment...

The era as a whole

There was a white façade

Bathed in light...

Which unfolded its name...

In black lettering...

Bar in a first room

All in length...

Dancefloor...

Kind of arena...

Cabin in height...

A staircase led to...

A lower floor

Industrial décor...

Metal pipes...

Large copper panels

Stolen staircase...

Paris was performing...

Programming of the basement.

We sang...

White Square...

Rue de Lappe...

Albert de Paname

Was Turning Bal de Paris...

Crystal ball...

In full delirium...

Maybe nothing changes

Oh, really...

Apart from the landscapes

The surfaces...

Were deserts...

Planet...

Thanks to dynasties...

Behind columns

Unknowns...

Haphazardly...

Until the moons...

Aquatic...

Time in reserve

Quest...

Since the night...

Original...

To the confines

What we perceive

At every moment...
And I wondered
Near the Villa...

16

This chance would mean a trip

Beginning of an episode...

Perfecto, t-shirt...

At dawn a coffee...

Troubled nights...

Overlooking the sea

Achievements to come...

Idylls...

We talked in their ears.

On the other side...

And we saw...

In the distance...

Their capes curl up

Secrets...

Appearances...

We would rarely see them again

Like those characters from the Coast...

Erotic days...

There was a steep path

Bare beaches...

Slow suggestions...

Open car...

From Avenue du Levant

Coastal fence...

Scorching...

Their minds went like the current

Goes to infinity...

At night...

Sense of history...

Recycled time...

Consents...

Undisturbed

In this project...

For millennia...

Questioning...

Motion printing

Continual towards a future...

17

Dimensional wall...

Primary data

Perceptions...

We had been by their side

On another level...

Always...

If we wanted to admit...

That there were no estates

Prints of the naves...

Light wings...

And snippets of the era

The towers were invited

Bright...

Morning hours

Sometimes sleep...

Desire for consistency

I loved this strength

Anchored in the present...

Enjoyment that prevailed

Away from unreasons...

People who were hurrying.

Era, giant lions...

Video wall...

We wanted to catch up

Happiness, ecstasy...

Prowess...

Infinite...

Smoother...

Electronics

Capturing lightness...

In desires...

Cybernetics...

Virtual enjoyments

Million years...

Sprinkle the space...

There had been a civilization

The rest of the time...

Worlds...

Before our prehistory

Lines...

Through time...

On the roads...

A long time ago

Wills...

Flying papers

Maybe...

I was looking at the world...

And I was trying to distract myself.

A few hours...

Screens...

Always attractions

Attractions...

Being drifting...

In the afternoon...

At the climax...

Other freedoms would come forward

Innocuous...

Embrace...

She was walking there...

In the streets of apotheosis

That we had surveyed...

Like lovers...

There was no time...

Only to wait...

To be against each other

Somewhere...

It all seemed so far away...

I fell asleep late...

Orgasms of virtual modes

Desire to sublimate...

Empathy...

For androids...
Their synthetic loves
At first, robots...

19

Universal Archives

Initial versions

Temporal texture...

Virtualities...

Units from elsewhere...

Part of a larger dream

Deliberate...

I could see them...

Time on the lips.

And I fell asleep late...

Caressing magnitudes...

Like chanted words

Glows in the trees...

Between two planets...

They would be renewed...

Maybe we invented this course...

Maybe we get attached to this story

On these screens...

Which watered us

From so many images...

Sequences...

Observational data...

Research...

Which tell us the story

The extent...

Original feeling...

Presence in the world

Paths from nowhere...

Nights, in this thought

Linearity...

Slow cycles...

They were watching us

Temptation to create...

Desire to transcend

As an aside...
Irresistible virtuality
Universal versions.

20

Dimensional freedoms

Maybe dreaming...

Hours...

Like chanted words

Refinement...

Between two planets...

I gave myself time...

To extract from the pleasures

Immediate...

Expectations...

Fantasies

Unlikely...

Maybe...

Versions...

Original models...

They were mimicking...

Precisely our passions

Quick, a coffee...

Black, at dawn

Motley...

On screens.

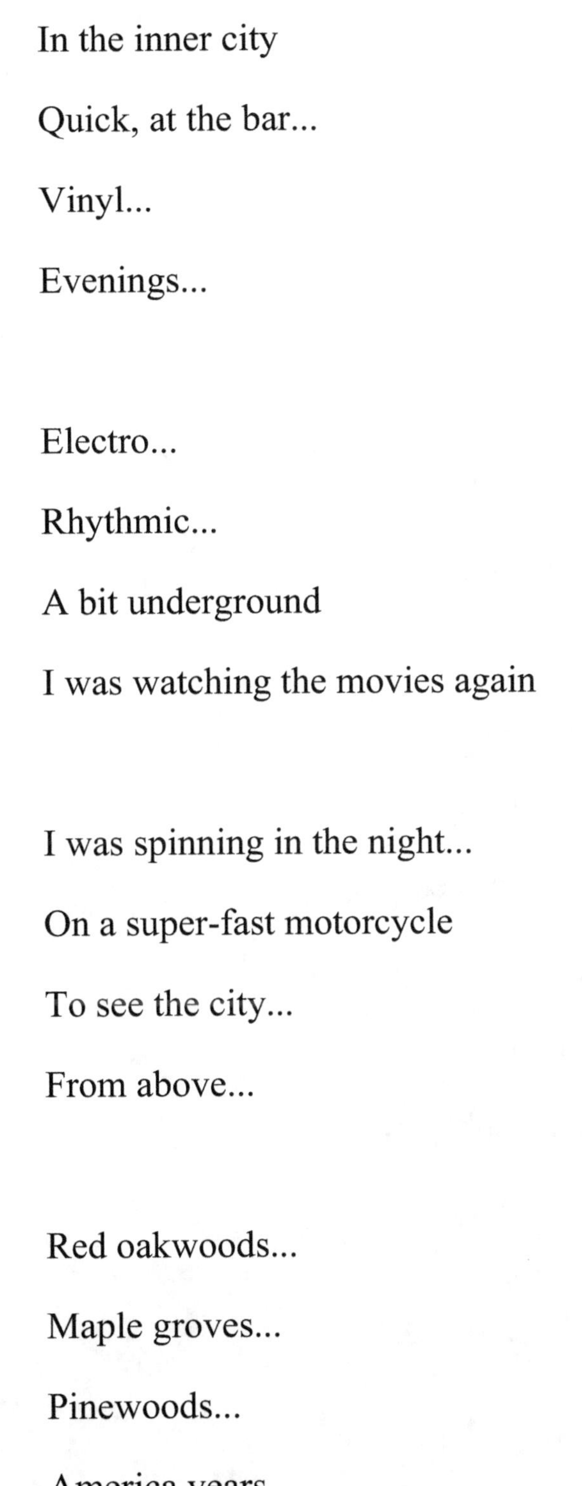

In the inner city

Quick, at the bar...

Vinyl...

Evenings...

Electro...

Rhythmic...

A bit underground

I was watching the movies again

I was spinning in the night...

On a super-fast motorcycle

To see the city...

From above...

Red oakwoods...

Maple groves...

Pinewoods...

America years.

21

Altitude...

By the ephemeral

Turns...

Kilometers...

In music

Dreamlike...

Empires...

The night flew by

White...

Trees...

Parking...

The days had passed

Like images...

Through the rows

I was interfering...

In the colors...

News...

Snippets of dance...

End of the evening...

I remembered the tall masts

Foliage...

And playful shadows

In slow motion...

Sleep of cities

Towers...

At night...

Quiet...

Smooth images

From my youth

Magic...

Perspective...

More dreams

A thousand lights...

In these hours...

Of total regeneration...

Twinkling, orange lights

Between the snow towers...

22

Installation...

Sleek design

Long evenings

On those nights...

Snow would slow things down

I'd pull out a few vinyls

I would think...

At other times

Bold...

To these advances...

Anyway...

And even if we never knew

The reason...

Planet...

Millions of years

To the landscapes...

Incredible...

Summer...

Climactic...

Precursors...

Mysteriously.

City guarded...

By colossi...

Of which we know nothing

Bluish halo...

Formerly...

With its pure walls...

Endless...

As an object of study

Glory...

From a completion...

That the spirit had extorted from matter

Momentum of a thought...

Emotion of the slopes...

Green...

We saw their rebirth

Mixing with time...

23

I had always loved them

Here, there...

At the end of the world...

In the look we exchanged...

One moment...

I had captured energy from all worlds

End of the lagoon strip...

Only boats...

Lights that stood out.

The years...

Swarming with stories

Prosperity, novelties

Cyborg lounge...

Ultra-perfect androids

Nightly conversations

Roboticist...

In search of adventure...

Martian...

Distant descendants...

Shadows and dust

Surfaces...

The exterior...

And our entrenchments

The effect of happiness...

Subtle impressions...

Retrospective layer

On everything...

First Martian...

Adventure...

Human capacity...

To be designed...

At night...

Perfection of time

And worlds...

Caresses of time...

There was in the moment

Eternal beauty...

24

Youth...

Hyperbolic power...

Infinitely

Mysterious smile...

Then I invited myself to this quiet feast

Fluid...

Month colors...

I had time ahead of me

Huge mirrors...

Students lost in their reading

Under a very high ceiling...

The days were beginning...

Snowy street...

A few years...

Corridors of a building

Granite avenues...

White spruce...

Olivier de Bohème...

American elm...

Corinthian style...

Marble from Belgium.

Niche cornice...

And stone balustrade...

Large hall...

Terracotta capitals

Gold leaf ceilings

Marble from Italy...

Winds and dust...

Sweeping the outside...

Like the silence of the centuries

Adventurous cities...

From that time...

From the world...

Attempts...

Spontaneity

Lines...

Fierce...

Journey

On the beach...

Des Chalets...

Ah...

They had clung to a dream

To an ideal...

Wandering charm...

No end, no limits...

In a corner of the spheres.

Field of herbs...

Red...

Formerly...

Beneficial walk

Between the towers...

For no apparent reason...

Variable page...

The ephemeral carpeted their nights

Platforms...

Flying cabins...

Like a second

Enough for travel.

In these waverings...

Dimensional...

Arid plains...

Modalities of the first case

Those who were there before them

Disseminating the supreme art...

At the exact points...

Had found the answer...

Lost...

Maybe passing...

Some abstruse plates

Sculptures...

Chapters...

Unexpressed wills...

Intact part of happiness...

We are in the flow.

26

One evening...

Since the time we observed them

Background of the ages...

We had met

One evening...

Song of hope...

Without expecting anything...

Voice to detachment...

Spatio-temporal bubbles.

Hyperspace...

Everything is so clear...

Beyond the sequences

Elusive forces...

Computers...

Incorporated into the material

Spiritual relays...

The pace became...

Glittering fir trees...

In the Square...

An air of Philadelphia

To others passions.

A few hours...

Pleasure to walk...

Desire to be in rhythm

From the night...

And I remembered...

Formerly...

Turrets...

We were driving to the coast

Midnight...

Reeling...

On this planet

Possible...

Whiteness of surfaces

Alchemist...

Fluid memory...

Retrospective...

27

Gentle and calm rides...

Glorious landscapes...

I remembered the energies

It was a pleasant time...

Sweatshirts...

Make music easy

We ventured on the roads

In the night...

Clubs deep in the woods...

Our desires...

In the car...

It took almost nothing...

The years created distances

Changed nature...

Distances...

Which turned into stories...

The present moment in every joy

Short story...

That moment was slipping away

Plan that was unfolding...

Travel back in time...

Postulate of causality

Complex...

Long suite...

Unlikely...

Appearance of principles...

In the same space-time

And adaptive purpose...

Twisted chains...

Coherence in motion...

Something came from further away

Complex relativity...

Two juxtaposed space-times...

Unification...

Punctual trace...

From a structure...

Housed in the imagination.

Space axes...

Gaze of Consciousness

And the gaze of Memory...

Every memory

In a universe...

Psychomatter

Human history...

Virtual intelligence...

Through time and space.

Initial version...

Could we create a universe...

Intended to be visited...

By those of us who would like to indulge

The stars would disappear...

Initial attractions...

Erotic distance at times

As we wanted...

To meet...

We were creating a poetic setting...

Virtual architecture...

That would have been placed in one of the pearls.

Deciphered by beings...

Advanced...

Transfer of information

By simple touch...

Platforms...

Altitude...

In the time of artificial skies

Green and gold...

A long time ago

Martian soil...

By downloading...

Consciousness...

Backup...

Recovery...

Digitisation...

Complexity.

29

Conquest of a space

Special dimension

Commune...

Capabilities...

Conversion

Space...

Light...

At night, intermediate

The time was different...

Timeline benchmark

Specific to spheres...

Old...

Inexhaustible centuries...

Now and then...

Busy enjoying...

To be merged...

Thirsty for taste

Fascinating reliefs...

Traveled in all directions

There were days...

Where we met.

We met again in the evening...

Days passed...

Like back and forth

Exquisite abundances...

Under high ceilings...

Or dreamed skies...

I indulged...

Ville-Marie des animations

It was dark...

Eyes met

Fairy evenings...

Time...

The fresh air...

In the streets...

Mini-adventures...

We whispered afterwards.

30

Subdued light...

Cold outside...

With the first snows

She took off her clothes

Bohemian...

The city was falling asleep...

The plot...

Future of the world

This color...

In the distance...

In the background...

Of their positions...

The unknown guided them

In the center of the bases...

Sealed...

In the place of the first visitors

Of those who had paved the way

We were watching them...

At the top of the towers...

Flags flew

Masts were soaring...

Horses of the Leonids...

And under the glow...

The images curved

Powdery days

The nights were long

Thoughtful...

The universes interposed

American style...

Panoramic...

Huge...

All kinds

Forest...

I remembered...

After the inauguration of the Space

Everything was different, of course...

We were young...

31

Summer had the rhythm

Of our embraces...

Scorching roads...

From Spain...

After the reeds...

A few months of loneliness

Endless beaches

At the detours...

Magical sanctuaries.

Necessarily magic...

Duration of existence...

Perceptions...

She came from the end of the city

From a windy island

Steps of a place...

Collections...

Works...

Under a vault...

The capitals...

The memories...

Escaped, smooth screens.

In a pile of leaflets...

There was all this history

The unfoldings...

And hope...

Landscapes...

Passions...

Reunited with wonders

Primary sources

In the colors...

Sometimes...

Things came by themselves

Were returning to their future...

Power increased tenfold...

She was looking at me a little...

Sketched a smile encompassing everything...

And our hearts, sensual forms at random.

32

Dose of joys...

Improvisation

And desires...

Where we rested...

The horizon, and the passing days...

That we hadn't counted

I would remember a summer

Years, light dresses...

Exhilarating youth...

At will...

Images of our loves

Of sand...

Spinning into the night...

Reviewing your look...

Land heat...

Always...

Indestructible images

Protective energies

Under the dome...

Regenerative...

A path...

The narration...

The next page

Like the days

Caresses...

A great year...

General color...

Formerly...

A technology would liberate

It was time that had flown

We had noticed...

Not attaching to our bodies

Nor to our minds...

Like life in a hurry captive

Between the palm trees...

The exotic pools...

To the ice...

33

Peninsula...

At the level of the white coasts

Between branches...

Through time...

Strings of movement...

How many possible moments

The moment as a triumph...

Beach dress...

The foliage had the dancing shade.

Towers, screens...

It was Bermuda time

Lights installed in the square

Fantasy on the snow...

Where we celebrated New Year's Eve

In 2044...

Cars were running...

Whenever...

We had replaced the drift...

Armored nomadism...

Cold cities...

And I would write all these things.

Life escaped from an illusion...

From a time that did not exist...

Coat of reality...

Which had started we did not know where

From cause to consequence...

That we organize in a leak of seconds

To make them look like a sequel...

Subjective...

Below a rocky road

In a cove...

They pointed to the island...

Transi of hibiscus...

Strip of sand...

Bathed in glow

Bypassing summer

Since midnight...

34

In the tain, our thoughts

Plots of eternity...

The evening of this world...

Theatres of an impetus

Founder...

I was looking at them...

On the other side of the cities

Spiritual machines...

Planetary happiness...

Roads of the schelems...

Which led us to the party

In other spaces...

Carefree...

Galaxy clusters would converge...

In huge, bigger galaxies

Speed of expansion...

From a universe...

We would pass far away...

We'd meet again...

We would remember the matches

Which we were witnessing...

Then we would go to a hotel

Stealthy caresses...

T-shirt, fluid dreams...

Fantasy...

Long carnival...

Alcoves...

Of our mysterious designs

Spring...

The same beauty...

The same green eyes

Memorabilia...

Long race...

Some summers...

Seaside...

On motorcycles...

Silk Road.

35

Billions of solar systems

Galaxy among billions...

Universe...

Life had emerged

Sooner or later...

On the beach...

Years...

Atmosphere of simple things

Pleasures of being together...

The country appeared modern

Unforgettable...

On a quiet road...

We were lucky...

Sometimes we stopped...

One day, I turned a hundred years old.

Everything had seemed far away...

Years had passed...

Earthly history...

One evening, staring at the screen

North American...

New restoration...

First visit of the king...

New World Order...

During the great confrontation

Hypnotic...

The nights had come...

Following the celebrations

In the heart of the waves...

Artificial...

At the top of the massif...

Years passed...

Centenarians would throw their swords

Space bunkers...

Cloning crowds...

And areas...

Assembly of the Old Men

Western...

36

Satellite wall

Missions to Mars

Low orbit...

Days with a crew

Cylinder with portholes...

Thrusters...

In the ship...

Pearl bracelet...

I'm somewhere else at the same time.

They told us they knew a shack

At the top of a rocky peak...

A mountainous region...

One day soon...

Wandering...

Dose of unrealities...

Over there...

At the end of a sky

Saturated with their vials...

Youth...

Leaving the grip of another magic

One evening...

It was a bit early at that time

Vague idea of the route...

I had seen her again...

On a quiet evening...

Top floor of a building

Nanominiaturize...

A copy of the key...

Virtual Architecture...

Beginning...

A new page

Intoxicating doors...

In both directions...

On the simple side of light

Under a slow sky...

We had many lives...

Martian...

37

Advanced Beings

Euphoric...

Camber...

Forest...

Music

Irreplaceable

Screens...

Erotic...

Vaguely clear.

Before daylight...

After nights...

Anything new

Indentation...

Each was the reflection

And we were linked...

By a decadence...

Ah...

We wanted to rave

Years passed...

For a while...

New life of the courses...

Youth...

From a romantic perspective

To renew itself...

Again and again...

Contours...

From the megalopolis...

And many other places

A very long time...

Hugs...

In the colours of the flag

With the people...

From the time...

New generations

In the arena of days

And time...

Unknown parties...

38

Stealthy caresses...

Mutual...

Suspicions of love

Then it would snow...

The world would go where it would like

Planetary wandering...

Blue gardens...

Enclosed terraces

From the world...

The space...

And the story...

The spheres...

Continuity

I remembered our youth

Clothes, perfume...

District...

We were waiting for the noises to end...

Undefined microcosm...

Anarchic wavelength

Lack of sleep...

By intrepid cadences...

Windows open to the courtyard

Deep car parks...

Partygoers with statements...

Thunderous...

Where I woke up...

Where I was shooting a little...

We had ridden at night

Snowy roads...

Stolen evenings

Hotel mirrors...

Bare pools...

Momentary...

In the holidays...

Azure...

She had a Tokyo look...

Short hours to fall in love.

39

Towers, gardens

In spiral version...

Beating airs...

In the streets...

Crowds...

Mavericks

Coincidences...

Cut off from hourds

Were steam...

In people's minds...

A change...

On the screens...

Like colors

Formerly...

Attraction parties

Empire...

To the surfaces

Planet...

For a thousand years...

Pioneers...

A new era.

Essential step...

Like other pioneers...

With advanced beings...

She would see a few of them

Ship back to Earth...

They were coming back from their memories

Almost dreams...

Long dust race...

There were hologram faces

Hyper-fast motorcycles...

Adventurous lifestyle...

After all the departures...

Buried moments...

We escaped from ourselves

On the roads...

Retro version...

40

I remembered...

That we drive at night...

A dense forest, music

We were talking about the future

Other celebrations...

Evenings of vials...

Coming back from elsewhere

Linger, ending the night

We listened to Lara Fabian...

And the city...

We had to blend in...

In other courses

Imagining other joys

Space station...

Long journey...

Low orbit...

For stays

Resources...

From Earth...

New habitats

Destination Mars...

Explorations...

Inhabited...

On the moons...

Three hundred and sixty days

More water than expected...

Different conditions...

Of those that had been imagined

Vast and long passages...

Mysterious...

Years of Martian presence

Platforms...

Since the time of heaven...

They dive...

Annihilate fatigue...

Bodies...

They used to sleep.

41

Mountain of cycles...

Energy...

There had to be a source

Infinite...

We see this liberated world

Modulations...

In the night...

She slipped into a flowing dress

Caressed with drunkenness...

To be only desires...

Inaccessible...

In another attractive light...

She dressed and undressed

Looking for herself too

To be herself...

Theatre of the century...

Red armchairs...

Long scarf around the neck

Short skirts...

Seaside...

And we fell in love...

Same novels...

Elongated books

On a mattress...

Blinds drawn...

One against the other...

Our differences were changing...

The stories took on eroticisms

Differed from the original attractions...

Cinemer, open-air...

Long beaches...

Near the pond...

We were hurtling down rocky slopes

And I was thinking about those years

Youths...

Yellowed leaves on the roof

At the back of the church...

42

I could see the neighborhood...

New places were created

New buildings...

Some nights...

Where I just had to let go of the hours

I gave the impression, those evenings...

Not to be rushed by things

To take my time...

In this time...

Holidays...

Fuss...

We crossed paths in the night

Searching...

Sensations...

Bare shoulders...

Just a stone's throw away...

Smart Square

Leaf swirl...

The place was alcove...

The birds flew between the trees

For a long time...

Youth...

Always...

The spirit of the times

Many years...

Chandeliers by chance...

Evening was coming...

Fidgeted on the other side

Towers...

Buildings were erected

Exotic images...

Melted in the morning...

In a dream...

In the evening...

I fell asleep late...

Unhurried, Asian...

In space-time.

43

Did we really know...

How things were changing

Part of latitude...

Nit...

Billions of years

On Earth...

Birds flew over trees

They were more slender...

We didn't notice...

They had powers

Strange...

City lights...

From my youth...

Near the park...

I decided the course

A few hours...

Dressed short...

For themselves...

Because they felt free...

Cities were a journey...

Looks, most of the time.

All this converged...

I was waiting for her...

The night was appearance

Truce, like a summer...

She looked like one of those actresses.

Films by Roy Stuart...

The air of nothing...

Fantasy, clothes from elsewhere...

Passing images...

We would talk about things

And others...

On the sand...

Formerly...

I wasn't looking for anything else...

That the present...

We were discussing the past days.

44

Sleepless night...

Trips...

And liqueurs

Various...

And the party faded

All this was far away...

I saw the place again...

As in the past...

On the radio, there was Wham!

Some cabins

Here and there...

The landscape...

The terraces...

Fuss...

Certainly...

Youths...

Looks

In the clear sky

Gardens...

Blue waves...

Years...

Our youth

Under an arch

Trips, at night

Hypnotic...

Never satiated...

To be against each other...

Blue net, long wet hair

The infinite...

I had walked near the ponds

And from the sea...

Route of boats...

Lights...

We guessed the vegetation...

Shaved...

And the water had gradually become closer.

On the beach of the Chalets...

45

The city from the top of the vineyards

With young colors...

Smiling path...

I mingled with the crowd...

Like in the past...

There would be this colorful atmosphere

Parisians would sing in the café

World Cup...

At night...

Everything was quiet...

Upstairs...

Tall trees quivered

In the wind...

I was spinning in the night

Ultra-fast motorcycle...

Dried leaves...

Kingdoms on the run

The sorrows and joys vanished

Under a winter sky...

Orange or purple...

Muses ...

On the paths...

The countryside was covered in snow

The dawn had its pleasant reflections...

By some ecstasy...

The immense weather had made us look strange

And beautiful...

Stories became other stories...

Were on other exciting ardours...

The thousand-year-old drunkenness...

And a clear latitude...

Which filled our souls

Quantity of atmospheres...

The cherry trees of Yasukuni–jinja temple were in bloom

It was time for the sakura...

Trees covered with millions of flowers...

It was the feast of ephemeral beauty...

46

Contemplation at Matsumae Castle

At Muramatsu Park...

Along the road to Nijukken...

Then summer came...

In the district of Kabukichō...

The atmosphere was clammy and overcharged

And we showed ourselves in finery

Towards the center of true desires...

In the great century that was coming...

We listened to Daft Punk...

Like a long time ago...

Mysterious and soaring pleasure...

Endless days and nights

Attractions...

Eroticism...

Still falling in love...

From our old illusions

The desire to let things go...

All this seemed to belong to other eras.

In other spaces...

Elixir of worlds and happiness...

That year...

In space-time breaches

Oh, really...

I had found old albums...

Blonde heroine...

Tidy eras...

Like gaits

Unforgettable...

Dimensions were displayed

Memory...

Sometimes...

Reveries and attractions...

Remember...

Very high speeds

Above a rail...

Propelled capsules...

47

Maybe all this had never happened...

Maybe this whole thing was a dream...

And maybe also that any story was yet to come.

Beginnings and dreams...

I remembered that time...

Her hair was floating in the wind

After the drought of summer...

Transparent tunic...

When we walked on the yellowed grass.

At the heart of the years

Dreams...

Roads...

Maybe...

Tracks...

Inspiration...

Hope beyond games

As the days go by...

Nights of reflection...

Horizons...

Opening up to the world...

Perimeter of a memory.

Carrying bags of emeralds...

Charged with atmospheres...

We remembered times gone by

And we were seeing future images...

I was thinking about all this...

When I wasn't really looking at the street

Vintage lamps that brought the spirit...

Lofts...

My gaze hovered...

And my memory recreated eras

Emotions...

Discoveries...

Premiums paces...

I gave myself a time...

Reflection...

I found old books.

48

Pleasant drunkenness...

And horizons revisited...

Energies of the deepest youth

Ah...

I had found old vinyls

I remembered a big pool

Very quickly...

Naked procession...

Magnetizations.

Years passed...

Months and years...

We walked in youth

The hours flew by...

Atmospheres, eras...

Somewhere, perhaps...

Without history...

We were moving away from yesterday

Snow course, the evening came...

Strange nights of dreams...

Other eras arose in dreams

Experienced by others, by ourselves...

As we were...

In fluid fabrics...

Ephemeral altitudes...

We talked about the future

Slow transformation

Consciences...

Stars...

There were lamps...

There were flowers...

For a moment

Many universes...

Months passed...

Epoch...

Love...

Drunken smiles...

In the distance the nightlife.

49

Century of experience

Nascent world...

In space...

Universe, universe...

There were worlds...

Within other worlds

Memories of worlds

Past or future...

Years more...

And we liked...

Joining the drifts

Landscapes...

Streets and beaches...

Our desires in the night...

Insolent day...

Overlay...

A few steps together

Between books...

Transparencies...

Chances...

Snow was announced.

Maybe this story

We had imagined it...

At night...

The hours of dreams...

Go around again...

Recreating pleasures...

Hopes...

I saw worlds

These times would sleep

In the mirrors...

And we would go to the source...

Unknown mirages...

Myriad worlds

Outstanding...

In the breaches...

Temporal...

50

We would like, we would like

In these moments...

Attractions of cybernetic oases...

More than ourselves...

Only simple sequels...

In the moment, like desires

Remember...

There was a staircase...

Which led to the choir.

Mosaic...

We hit the road

Southern...

An unbeatable summer...

In the distance, we guessed between the trees

Which soared to the sky...

The massive towers and turrets...

Thousands of words like spheres

Whirling...

Years had passed

Flakes, lost hours

There was snow...

We would read in the memory...

And I returned without hurry...

I gave others time for things

The sauteries, for a period of time...

See parties...

Barely finished...

The rhythm of her gestures...

And stop at the climax

Fantasies to regenerate...

The youth of the attractions...

Force that interfered with desire

Rehearsals of chapters...

We were trained...

Through unreal images

We crossed paths...

By chance...

51

The cottage was purple...

We hurried

To hug us...

Before loving our story more

Skilfully...

Over there...

All the time...

Turns were arranging

Our air by the way...

Starry sky...

To the Sailing School

Dark sea and waves...

Invisible...

Imagining stories

The birds sang

In the clear sky...

And would leave soon...

I would remember a summer

Exhilarating leaflets...

There was all this history

The unfoldings so long...

I had recognized some terrain

Some fields...

A dry stream...

Beyond the time...

A long time ago...

I remembered that I was spinning

Outrageous currents...

Holiday lanterns...

Ocean...

Paname...

Between classes

Languages...

And her perfume floated...

In the alcohol of the trips...

The square looked like a park

Attractions...

52

Village of festivals...

I had wanted to taste...

With millennial atmospheres

There were in those hours

Love...

Greatness...

The heart of our youth

It was simple...

At the birth of the waves...

Between shrubs...

And brambles...

At the end of a bend

Steep...

Headland...

Which dominates the sea

Bewitching cove

Sublime sailboats

On the warm sand...

Walking on the notes

I saw these acres...

Pure joy...

Around a star...

On the surface of a planet

Potential...

Certainly rocky...

Transition...

Near...

Mini-Neptune...

Earthly nature

Probable...

Atmosphere...

The heat...

Around the planet

Life possible...

On more areas

Exoplanet...

From a calm host star...

53

The star...

Very long period

Rotation...

Atmosphere...

Chances of habitability

Billions of years...

Similarity...

With the Earth...

Strange landscape.

A few wakes...

In the background of the decor...

Automatic colors...

Maybe sleeping plans

The ink...

Running on paper...

A nothing, the feeling

To be in flyover...

And this landscape...

The plot...

Life...

Last rampart.

The unifying door...

And the summer that comes

Intoxicating gold...

Nomads...

Human project...

To be free...

And now comes the time

Under the sky...

I remember a road

Endless...

Because I was so young...

Calm Asian memory...

Adulation...

Currents...

Audacious...

Kinds of naves.

54

In the ether...

New people

A thousand years away...

I was there...

Yesterday...

Appearances

I had already had to tell

All this history...

The landscapes change...

What happens to sailboats

Hours in parallel...

In the evening of another corner...

Colors out of the blue...

Things were going by themselves

Way of the reeds...

Waves...

Everything seemed possible...

Possible course of drunkenness

Elsewhere...

Sublime passages...

Maybe...

There were dials

Screens...

The wheel...

Time on the lips...

Between us and the future...

He was coming back from a space

Purely imaginary...

Aphrodisiac...

We had all run together...

The branches rose to the sky

Nested dimensions...

Fluid tissues...

Interfering in the opening

From a curve...

Intoxicating foam...

Maybe appeasement...

55

Nomadic imagination...

Mirages of our hearts

Walks...

Attenuating high voices

Around the gaze...

Aftermath...

Triumphs in memory

While away the hours...

The interludes...

Time gave us back this rhythm

Now and then...

Recreated space...

In the distance...

Carpet of leaves...

Whirling...

In slow motion towards the square...

Enthusiastic young faces

Bright image...

In the meditative advance

There was momentum...

In the evening...

In the rustic living room...

So many memories emanated

From the city...

Stories...

In chocolate perhaps...

Maybe just that...

Remember...

You felt like you were alone

Then we tried to slow down...

And we were trying all sorts of things...

The night sparkled...

These precious eras are gone

After many scrolls...

I don't know where...

There were parties...

Glass and light towers.

56

Shining Star of the Future

In the passage of time...

Maybe other joys...

It was snowing...

I was tapping the rhythm...

Where we had decided essential things

A row of atmospheres...

More time...

There, the world, the tirades.

Touching...

Blurred moments

In low shave...

A road...

A hotel...

White...

Season of passage

The reeds...

For a long time...

The castles...

That I could make reappear

By thought...

The trees were lit

By the red lights...

Which came out of the sidewalks

From the neighborhood...

A very long time ago...

Maybe in another life

I had known her double...

In the middle of the reeds...

From the nature reserve

From the pond...

Lagoons...

Coots...

Facing the sea...

And looking at the horizon...

I remembered the years

Around secret beaches...

57

Fences with holes...

Seaside ...

The coves called

We had managed to stay alone...

A few hours...

It seemed to me that only a moment had passed.

The oceans would disappear...

Galaxies would merge

Billions of years...

Slow transformation...

From the universe...

Iguanas seemed to have come

From another age...

Dream in a library...

Maybe we had a random relationship

Which unfolded from our dreams...

And I was looking at the top of the towers...

Top of a cliff

Relaxing...

The night would pass...

Magic...

Amphitheater peripherals

Screens...

Dresses...

Fluids...

Arches...

From the seaside

By the runs...

At dawn...

Strange...

Hypnotic...

Promises of euphoria

Between continents...

Distant planets...

Since my early youth...

After a few sleepless nights

I was crossing...

Until thirsty...

Repetitive whirlwind...

Right in the spotlight

Getaways...

Endless...

Subtle imprint of glories

Memories...

Thinning...

Night show.

The gold of dreams

Bright...

Emancipated...

In the evening...

Days and nights flew by

I remembered the drunkenness...

The terraces...

Eternal and infinite desire...

Yesterday, I was crossing mirrors

Reservoirs of letters...

With the sea...

The capitals...

Dizzying atmospheres

Nocturnal cobblestones, chance

In classic mode...

Turrets...

I thought the party was moving

In our footsteps...

And I was thinking about the reflections...

In the present...

Scattered moments...

Appeasement...

Centenarians will cast their swords

Space bunkers...

Satellite wall...

Shopping...

With the landscapes...

Timepieces of a few dreams.

59

We loved the heart of time...

And we loved being able to start over endlessly.

Eternal regains, eternal hope of endless love

Some soaring views

Processions...

New deals...

In search of nothing...

Or maybe a magic

After all...

Strings of movement...

How many possible moments

And our worlds...

Pride...

Leaves...

Dials...

Distances...

Shortcuts

In opiums...

Screens...

Juggling the new city...

I remembered our wet necks.

Our adventures didn't have to be true

Illusions about the square...

Opium of the firmament...

Expectations...

Vials...

Elixirs...

Of paper...

Anachronistic

We were looking to direct our diligence

Garden horses...

Inviting codes...

Of triumphs...

Sequences...

Thought migrates...
Neutral spaces...
In virtual continents.

60

This light comes from elsewhere...

Snow covered the surrounding roofs

And he could fall asleep on it...

After a few hours...

Because even powerful interests are dethroned

Through sleep...

To the sound of consonants...

Affricated...

Sailing feasting proliferation.

At the foot of the statues...

Yellowed leaves...

Crazy curves...

I opened high gates

Overlooking the turret...

From a castle disappeared...

Overlooking a cove

In the sights

Of plants

And I heard...

By the drowned thrill...

A techno diatribe.

Party feel

Improvised...

Chandelier of the shores...

Impressive...

And I loved bedtimes...

And that purple halo...

I could see the skyscrapers...

By exchanging our thoughts

And there were the forgotten of the holidays

The Ferris wheel...

We would dance near the shores

Metaphorical cloud...

Northern Lights...

At night, cameras...

Beam color

Bright...

Projected light

Northern Lights

Interactive...

Flakes...

Hours lost...

We were going towards time

Inexhaustible...

And I remember the thread of the night

From the caress of shadows...

Doors slammed...

In haste...

It was the perfect weather

Simultaneity...

Celebrations...

Tropical...

Streets dotted with posters

In relief...

I was only traveling

At dawn...

Smiling...

Exotic roads...

Roman roads...

Nearby towers...

Ancient times seemed to us

As resources...

Propitious path

Broad strokes...

Of an existence

Gold projects...

Passions...

From the unforgettable center

From our beginnings...

Under the sky of a winter...

From so many shores...

I remembered thousands

Urban metaphor...

From a field...

Reflection of light...

Projectors...

Wheat ripples in the countryside

Ice floe...

Succession of arches

From tunnels...

Journey of an iceberg...

Polar waters...

Flakes, lost hours.

Perhaps the faces of youth

And that past loves were invited...

In my memory...

Distant silk roads...

Roads that crossed the fields

There were attractions...

By exchanging our thoughts...

At first, maybe at the beginning...

Lives and things...

Speed and power defined this era.

Added to the real ...

In space and time...

Millennia of rapprochement

Invisible connivance...

Based on enthusiasm...

And rehearsals...

We remembered the centuries

Previous...

Free memory...

The appearance of a party...

We were looking for the way...

Towards other dawns...

Rebirth...

There had been so many days and nights

Discover spaces...

There is still a taste from elsewhere

We must hope in other projects...

Others ourselves...

First versions...

Until the end of the global adventure

Spirit of an expanding world...

More millennia, this is the time

Curvatures, infinite passages...

We were traveling within ourselves...

And we were learning to think that it was so.

That the order of things was akin to a sequence

When everything was quiet...

Future wills...

On the horizon...

The giants of the future

Anchored...

Robots were responsible for drawing

The resources...

To create...

Small pits in the northeast...

Many planetary moons

Hypnotic approach...

In the heart of the evenings...

Course and advances...

How many mental constructs

Were we happiness...

As time shrouded us

Powers...

Like wearing a coat...

Magic...

We attended the establishments

Of everything...

Quasi-circular trajectory

Embedded progressions...

Some mystical light

On the outskirts and borders

The plan and the extension continued...

We were going back in time...

Quiet neighborhoods...

Lots of wood and raw materials.

67

To blend in...

In new times

There were corridors...

That connected places

Festive atmospheres

Transparent vials

We searched by thought

Habitable planets...

Near the large windows...

Near zinc...

Relaxed silhouettes

Coming and going since dawn...

I settled into the narrative...

With a kind of slowness...

Beneficial...

Inviting me into the pages...

To protect me from worn-out daily newspapers

There was a rocky exoplanet...

In orbit around the habitable zone of its star...

Red dwarf in the constellation Canis Minor

Super-Earth about three times the mass of Earth...

The advantage of orbiting a quiet host star

There were icy worlds...

Even more distant colonies...

A hope of rebirth...

Infinite...

On endless journeys...

Minds and bodies attracted...

The festival of yesteryear gave us routes of discovery

We were trying to feel in a moment

Out of the rest, the distant force...

A whole era...

Of joy, and our carefree embraces...

And in an instant, I saw the glow again.

Emerging...

So unknown wonders...

And ecstasies...

In the invigorating air...

From the beginnings...

Friends were arriving on skateboards

Blond moments...

Drunk...

In how many mirages

Magnetic attractions

Like a decor...

Serene intervals...

Propelled into the future...

Like volleyball players...

A few flakes...

There was the horizon in how many futures

We wanted to know a reassuring path

Mirific...

Extrapolation of dreams...

Infinite space, tall grass...

Crazy mental projections...

Of all that could have been done

Like the trips...

We didn't know where...

The tall trees...

Waves of desires...

Like immense happiness...

That we could not live identically again

The night would pass

As in the past

Magic...

Attraction...

There was eternal enthusiasm

Roads, in the distance...

In the passage of time...

Maybe...

Other joys...

In how many spaces...

Minimal adornments, forget the logic

At the bar of alcohol in a hurry...